# How Toys Work

Lisa Greathouse

# How Toys Work

## Publishing Credits

**Editorial Director**
Dona Herweck Rice

**Associate Editors**
James Anderson
Torrey Maloof

**Editor-in-Chief**
Sharon Coan, M.S.Ed.

**Creative Director**
Lee Aucoin

**Illustration Manager**
Timothy J. Bradley

**Publisher**
Rachelle Cracchiolo, M.S.Ed.

**Science Consultant**
Scot Oschman, Ph.D.

***Teacher Created Materials***
5301 Oceanus Drive
Huntington Beach, CA 92649-1030
http://www.tcmpub.com

**ISBN 978-1-4333-0307-4**

Printed by: 51497
Printed in: China

# Table of Contents

# Inside Your Favorite Toy

Do you have a favorite toy? It may be a stuffed animal that you got when you were a baby. Or maybe it is a cool race car. It might be a special doll. Or your favorite toy might be a robot.

Many toys can do things. A toy car has wheels and rolls. Many dolls have arms and legs that move. Some can even talk. Many electronic toys have lights and make sounds. There are high-tech toys that have mini computers inside them.

You might not think of toys as machines. But if you took apart a toy, you would probably find a machine inside! Some machines have a lot of parts and can do complex things. **Simple machines** do just one thing. They allow us to push or pull things more easily. Things all around your house use simple machines to make them work—and that includes many of your toys!

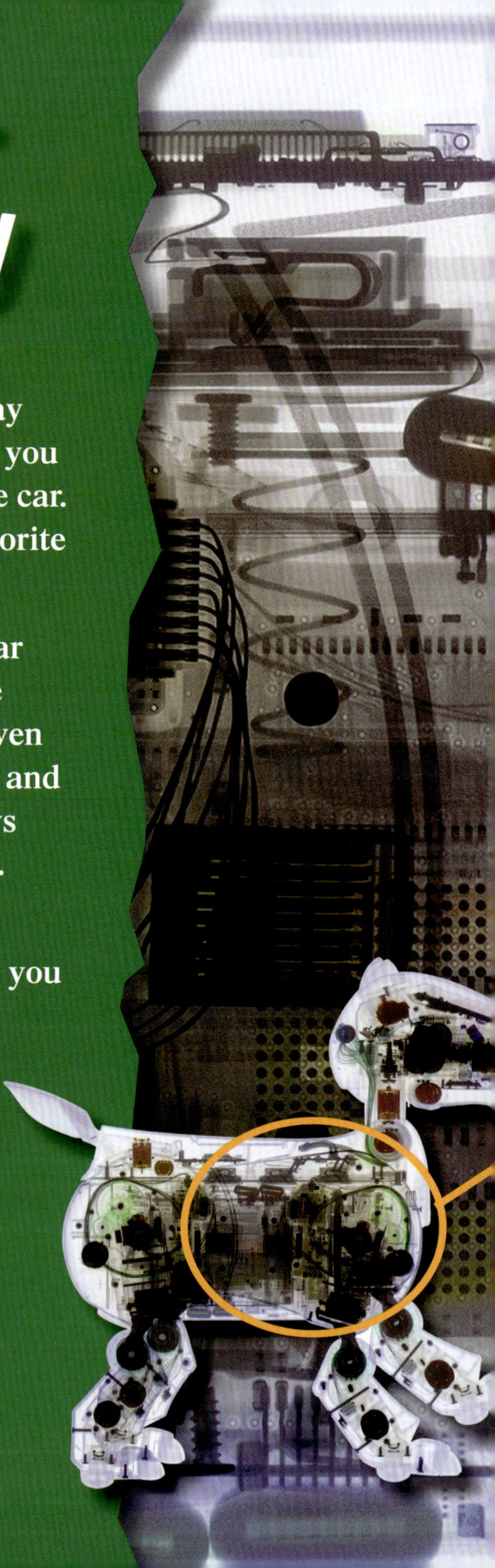

The enlarged image shows the inside of this robotic dog.

the first Barbie doll from 1959

## Best Sellers

Dolls have always been the top-selling toy for girls. Barbie is the best-selling toy of all time! Video games top the list for boys.

# The Science of Toys

You might not think that toys and science are related. But the truth is, science has a lot to do with how toys work. You might have some toys that do things that seem impossible. Toys like these are fun to play with. But it is also fun to figure out how they work.

Have you ever spelled words on your refrigerator with letters that have magnets on the back? Or played with darts that stick to the bullseye with a magnet? You have also probably played with many toys that have magnets inside them.

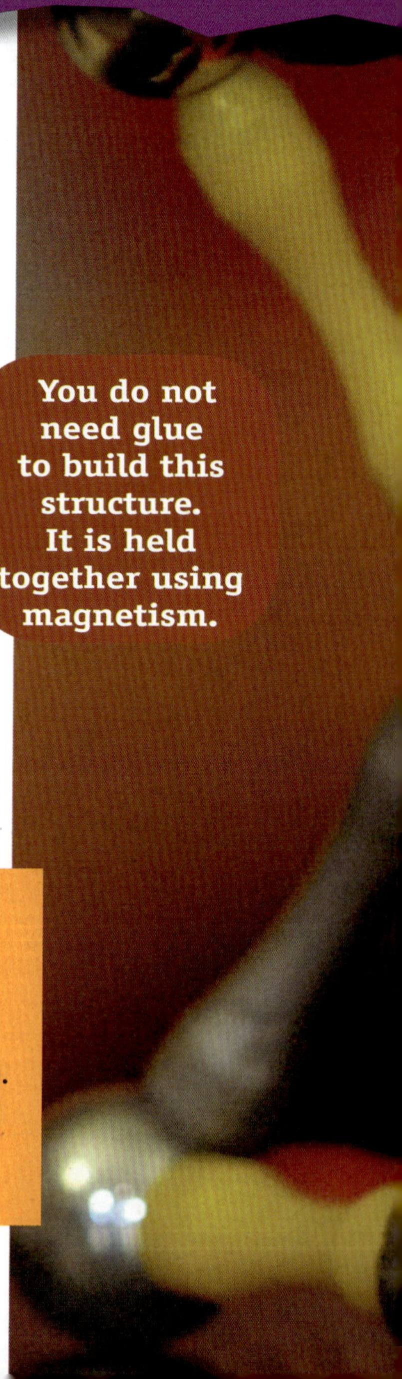

You do not need glue to build this structure. It is held together using magnetism.

## How Magnets Work

The pull or push that you feel when you hold a magnet is an invisible force called **magnetism**. Magnets are usually made of iron ore, or a metal that has lots of iron in it, such as steel.

The gauss is named after German mathematician and physicist Carl Friedrich Gauss.

## Gauss What?

Some magnets are strong, and some are weak. Magnetic fields are measured by a unit called a gauss. A refrigerator magnet is about 100 gauss. Scientists can produce magnets as strong as 40,000 gauss. The magnetic field of a typical neutron star is over 100 trillion gauss!

# The Strongest Magnet

A rare type of neutron star called the magnetar has the strongest known magnetic field in the universe. Magnetars are so strong that they could rearrange the **atoms** in your body! Only about 10 magnetars have been discovered so far. But scientists say there could be thousands of magnetars in our Milky Way galaxy.

NASA illustration of a magnetar

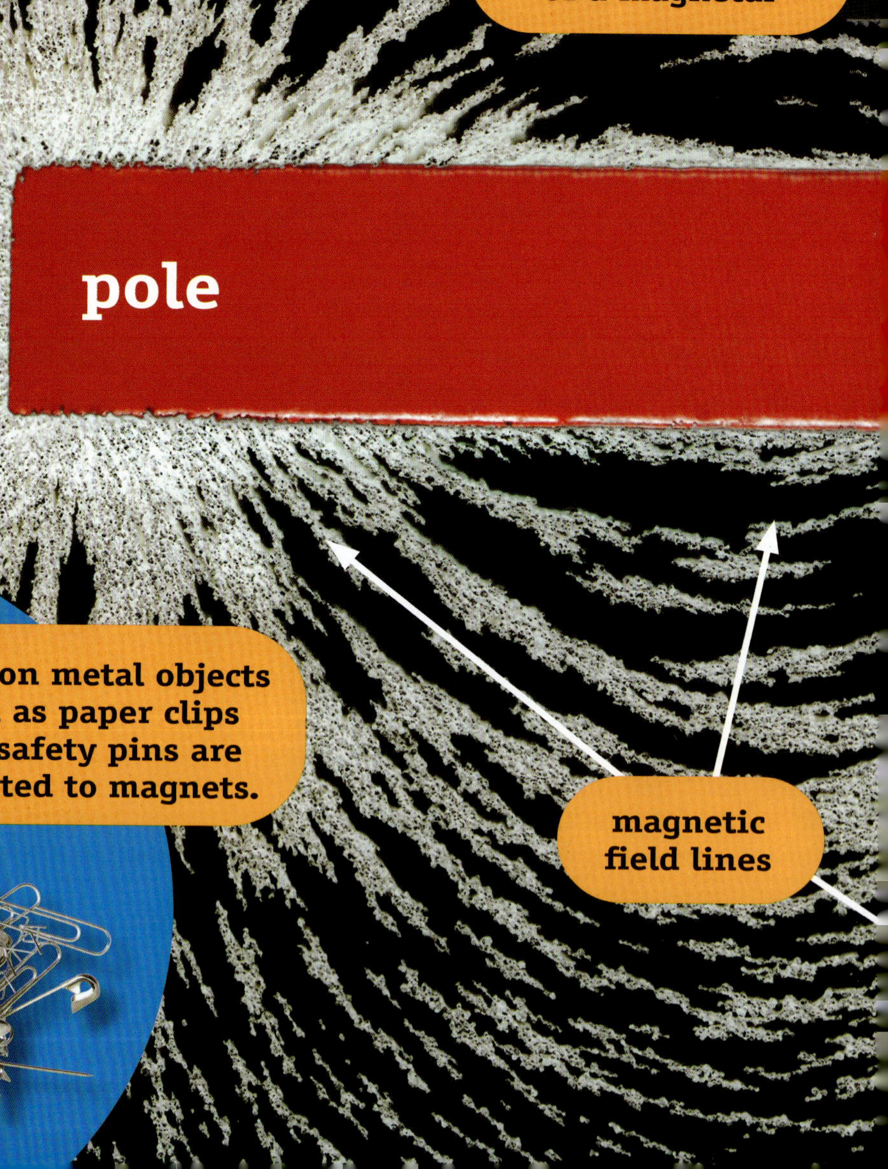

Common metal objects such as paper clips and safety pins are attracted to magnets.

# Opposites Attract

Magnets come in many shapes and sizes. All magnets have magnetic spaces, or fields, around them. The field will pull toward metals made of iron, steel, nickel, or cobalt. If you have ever picked up paper clips with a magnet, then you have seen a magnet make something move without ever touching it.

The ends of a magnet are called **poles**. Every magnet has a north pole and a south pole. They look the same, but these poles are opposites. If you hold the south pole of one magnet to the south pole of another magnet, you will feel them push apart (**repel**). But the north and south poles will pull toward each other (attract). In magnets, opposites attract.

Some magnets are very strong, and some are weak. A weak magnet might not even stay on your refrigerator. A really strong one might be able to move a refrigerator!

Magnets are found in things we use every day. Computers use magnets. Cell phones use magnets. Many of the toys you play with use magnets to make their parts move.

# All Charged Up

Have you ever opened a toy but could not use it right away because you did not have the batteries it needed? Toys that need batteries run on electricity. Some toys can be plugged into electrical outlets. Electricity is a form of energy, and it makes things move. It is made when tiny electrical particles called **electrons** interact with each other.

Electric charges come in two forms: positive and negative. Positive electric charges are attracted to negative charges. Negative charges are attracted to positive charges. Charges that are the same repel, or push away, from each other. Electric charges act like magnets in this way. Just like with magnets, opposites attract.

Have you ever felt a static electric shock? That is an electric charge. If you walk across a carpet, electrons move from the rug to you. Now you have extra electrons, and that makes a negative static charge. If you touch something, like a doorknob, the electrons move from you to the knob. Zap! You feel a shock!

When hairs build up the same static charge, they repel each other.

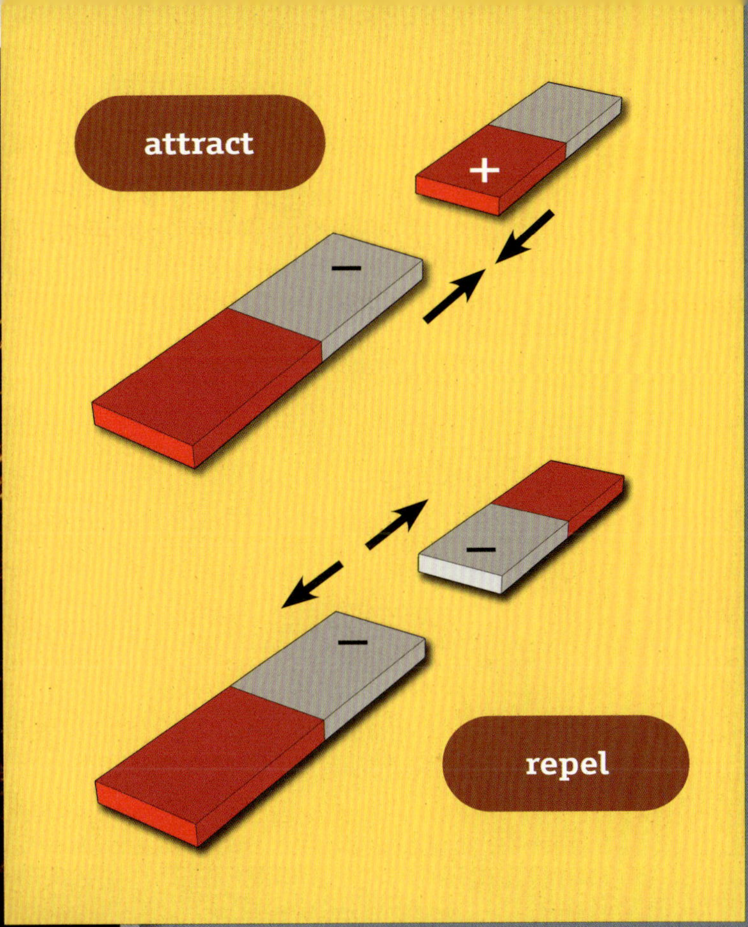


Some toys have complicated electrical systems.

# Simple Machines

You probably think lifting a heavy backpack is hard work. Well, you are right! In science, **work** is when a force moves an object. A **force** is a push, pull, or twist that makes things move. So pushing, pulling, and lifting are all types of work. Gardeners are doing work when they pull weeds. Shoppers are doing work when they push carts in a grocery store. Furniture movers are doing work when they move heavy boxes. It is even work when you cut a piece of pie! Simple machines make all these jobs easier.

There are six types of simple machines: the lever, the inclined plane, the wedge, the screw, the pulley, and the wheel and axle. They all make it easier to move things.

A bicycle is an example of a compound machine.

## Compound Machines

Compound machines have two or more simple machines working together. They can do more difficult jobs than simple machines alone. Almost every machine you see is a compound machine.

| Simple Machines | How it Helps Us | Examples |
|---|---|---|
| ever | lifts or moves loads | seesaw, bottle opener, hammer, shovel |
| nclined plane | lifts or moves loads | ramp, stairs, slide |
| vedge | cuts or splits, pushes away | axe blade |
| crew | holds things together | screw, jar lid, bolt, drill, light-bulb base |
| ulley | raises or lowers a load | mini-blind, flagpole, crane, tow truck |
| vheel and axle | moves loads | wagon, doorknob, pencil sharpener |

# Building the Pyramids

Experts think that the early Egyptians created ramps out of dirt to move huge stones when they were building the pyramids. Those may have been some of the earliest inclined planes ever used to make work easier.

Have you ever tried lifting a heavy box up a flight of stairs? It is much easer if you have a ramp to push it up instead. A ramp is an example of an **inclined plane**. It is a flat surface that is slanted. This simple machine can help you move objects more easily.

A **lever** is one of the most common simple machines. A seesaw is a type of lever. When you push down on one end, the force makes objects turn around a point and lifts whatever is on the other side. Almost anything with a handle is a type of lever, too. Think of how a hand shovel makes it easier to pry weeds out of the ground. All kinds of shovels are types of levers. They make work easier.

The pointed edge of an inclined plane is called a **wedge**. You can use it to push things apart or split objects. The blade of an axe or a knife is a wedge.

**Screws** are used to build things and hold things together. A screw really is like a little ramp that winds around with a wedge at the tip. Every turn of the screw helps move the piece of metal through a piece of wood.

Pulleys are used to lift or move things. In a pulley, a rope wraps around a wheel with grooves in it. When you pull the rope, the wheel turns. Any objects that are attached to the rope are moved. For example, pulleys are used to raise and lower flags on flagpoles. On the far right, a giant pulley moves chairs on a ski lift.

wedge

## Ups and Downs

Every time you raise or lower your window blinds, you are using a pulley.

pulley

screw

wheel and axle

## Gear Up

The gear is sometimes considered a simple machine. But it is really just a wheel with teeth.

Have you ever pulled something heavy in a wagon? Then you have seen how a **wheel and axle** make work easier. The wheels on the wagon turn the rod connected to them. That is the axle. When the wheels and axle turn together, it makes the wagon move. Wheels and axles also make bicycles and roller skates move.

All simple machines create **motion**. Motion is how, where, and why something moves. How something is pushed or pulled changes the way it moves. The wagon being moved by the wheel and axle can move in a straight line. But it can also move back and forth. It can move in a zigzag or even round and round in circles. If you get inside of it and bounce around, it will even vibrate! The motion of the wagon all depends on you.

The first rocking horses were made in ancient Egypt and Greece. This rocking horse is from the early 20th century.

## Shake, Rattle, and Roll

Rattles have been popular baby toys for hundreds of years. Early rattles were carved from wood and had seeds or even teeth inside to make noise when they were shaken. Today's rattles are usually made from plastic and have beads inside. But the way rattles work and the sounds they make have not changed over time.

# How Do Toys Work?

Many of the toys that your grandparents played with when they were young are much different from your toys. But you might be surprised to find that you and your grandparents—and even their grandparents—played with many of the same toys, as well.

Have you ever been on a rocking horse? That has been a favorite toy since the 18th century. Many older rocking horses were made of wood. Some had springs. Today, many are made from molded plastic. But almost all rocking horses work the same way: The child sits on the horse's back and holds onto the handlebars. Then the child uses his or her feet to rock back and forth. The energy moves the curved rocker on the bottom or the springs attached to the horse. That makes the horse move back and forth. The faster the child moves, the faster the horse moves.

Many playgrounds have rocking horses on springs, such as this one.

# Toys That Whir, Bop, and Talk

Many toys that have stayed popular over the years work in interesting ways. They may roll, spin, or float. They may have pieces of different sizes and shapes that can be used to build things. They may have screens that allow pictures to be created just by touching them. Many toys make sounds, and some even talk. Sometimes it seems as if toys use magic to work!

Some toys, such as video-game systems, have compound machines inside them. Most toys that make sounds or move on their own run on electricity. But some have simple machines inside them that allow them to run with only the energy that comes from the child playing with them. Think about a toy car that zooms across the room after someone pulls it back and lets it go. This toy has a spring inside it that is wound tight when the car is pulled backward. When it is released, the energy from the spring is released as well. The more the car is pulled back, the farther it goes.

# An Accidental Toy

Have you ever seen a Slinky "walk" down a flight of stairs? The Slinky's inventor was trying to build a spring that would keep ship instruments from vibrating. One day, his experiment walked off a shelf and down onto the ship's deck! He knew that the spring would be fun to play with. Today, the Slinky is one of the best-selling toys of all time.

A spring and a compound machine make this robot walk.

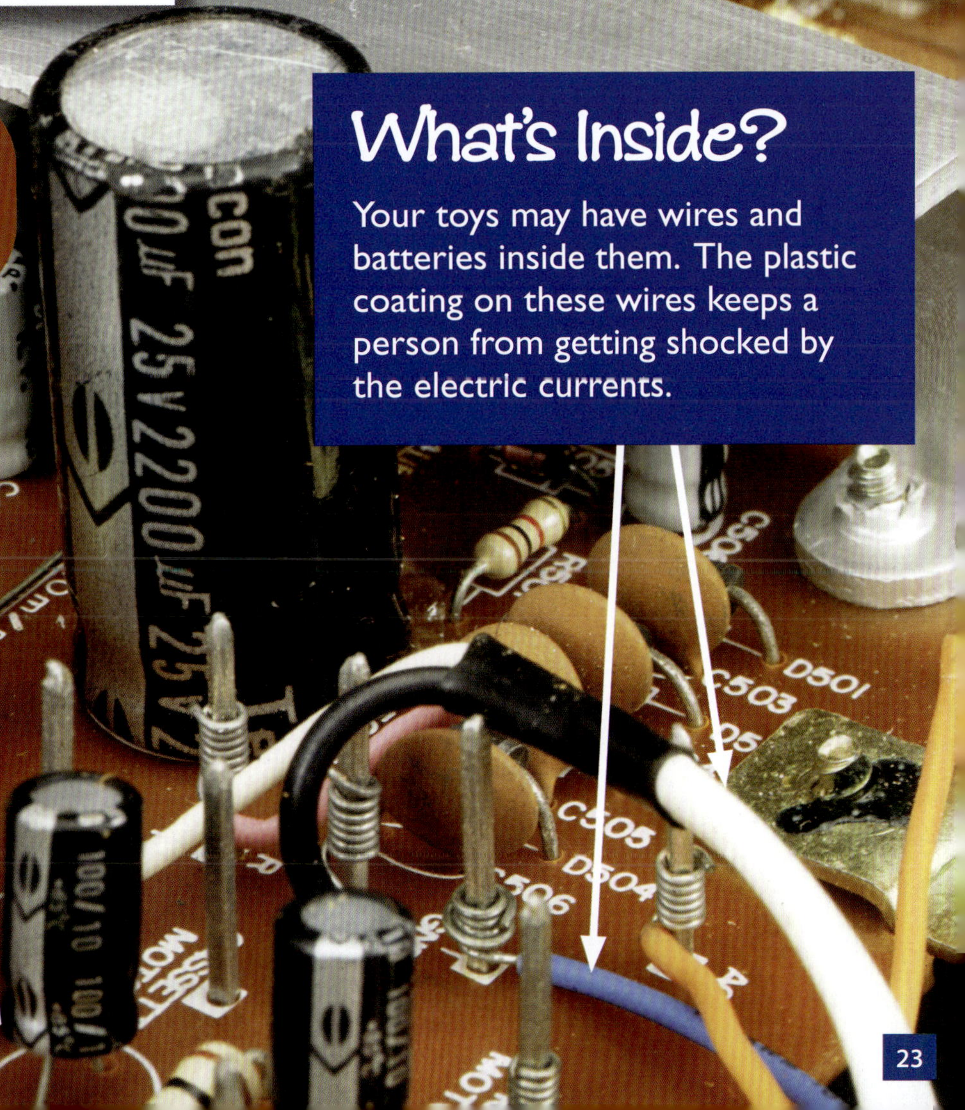


## What's Inside?

Your toys may have wires and batteries inside them. The plastic coating on these wires keeps a person from getting shocked by the electric currents.

# The Science of Spin

Can you think of any popular toys that spin? There are the spinning top, the yo-yo, and the Frisbee—just to name a few. When you throw a football in the air or spin a basketball on the tip of your finger, they become spinning toys, too.

Children and adults have been playing with yo-yos for hundreds of years. The yo-yo seems like a simple toy. But it is not quite as simple as it seems!

The simple machine inside of a basic yo-yo is an axle. It is connected to the round body and the string. When the yo-yo falls, it changes one form of energy to another. When the yo-yo is at the end of the string, it is spinning. That energy makes the yo-yo pull itself up on the string. Since some energy is lost on the way up, the player needs to add energy

## What Does Yo-Yo Mean?

The yo-yo was developed in the Philippines. A businessman brought it to the United States in the early 20th century. The name "yo-yo" was explained by some as the Filipino word for "come-come" or "to return."

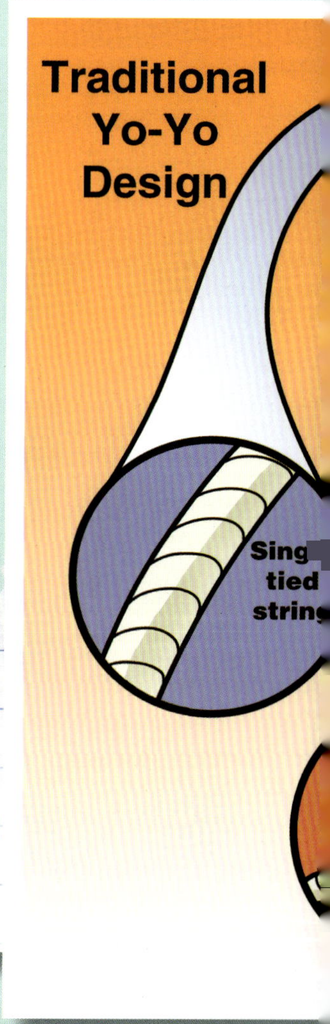

The original yo-yo had a string that was tied to its axle. The newer design has a string looped around the axle. This allows the yo-yo to do tricks.

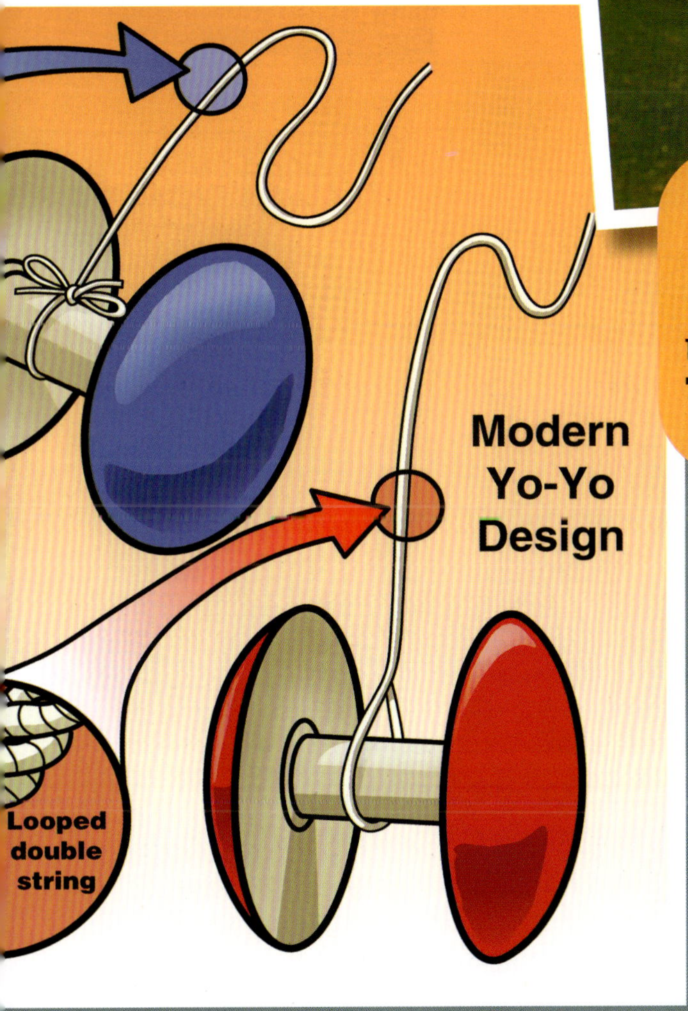

## Not the Easy Way Out!

Most people look for the easiest way to do things. But a Rube Goldberg machine is just the opposite. It is a machine that performs a very easy task in the most complicated way. Rube Goldberg actually drew funny cartoons of machines like these. Today, there are contests for people to come up with the "best" Rube Goldberg machine!

Working together, students build and test a prototype.

This compound machine has the simple job of squeezing fresh orange juice.

# Could *You* Invent the Next Big Toy?

If you could see inside your favorite toy, what do you think you would find? An electric motor? Wheels and magnets? Screws and springs? Or maybe a computer?

Toy inventors are always looking for ideas for the next great toy. First, they figure out what they want their toys to do. Then they draw pictures of how they want their toys to look. They decide what parts they need. Then they build models of the toys, or **prototypes**. This is a good way to test a toy and find out how to make it better. Toy companies usually have a team of people who work together to make a new toy.

Have you ever thought of an idea for a toy? Many toy inventors are **engineers**. Others study art. These days, many of them are computer experts. If you like to dream up great ideas, inventing toys might be the right career for you.

# Lab: Make Your Own Pinwheel

A pinwheel is an example of a simple machine. It is basically a wheel and an axle. A pinwheel uses wind as an energy source to make it spin.

## Materials

- a sharpened pencil
- scissors
- white construction paper
- ruler
- a paper fastener
- a plastic drinking straw
- crayons, colored pencils, or markers

## Procedure:

1. Cut a piece of construction paper into a 17.5 cm x 17.5 cm (7 inch by 7 inch) square.
2. Decorate both sides of the paper with crayons, markers, or colored pencils.
3. Place a ruler diagonally from one corner of the square to the opposite corner. Follow the diagonal line of the ruler and draw a 7.5 cm (3 inch) line toward the middle. Repeat this for each corner, so that you have four lines drawn toward the middle.

4. Draw a small circle to the left of each line, near the edge of the paper.

5. Cut along each line, but try not to cut all the way into the center.

6. Pull each corner into the center and make the four circles meet at the center of the square.

7. Push the end of the paper fastener through the circles. Push the fastener through the center.

8. Use the sharpened pencil to poke a hole through the straw that is about 1.25 cm (.5 inch) from the top.

9. Place the straw on the backside of your pinwheel and push the ends of the fastener through the hole in the straw. Open the fastener by flattening the ends in opposite directions.

10. Now all you need is a little breeze to make your new pinwheel spin.

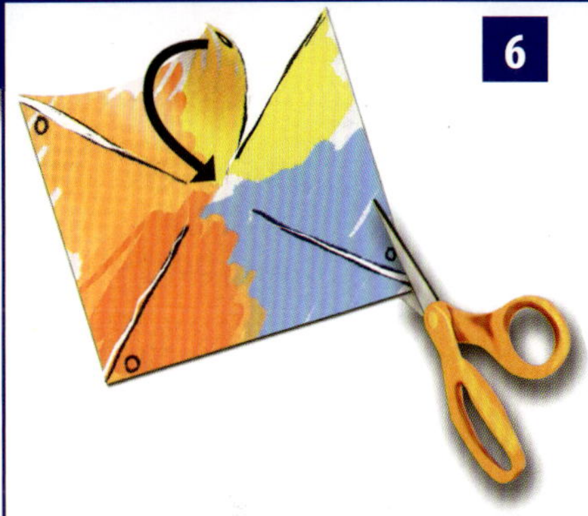

6

7

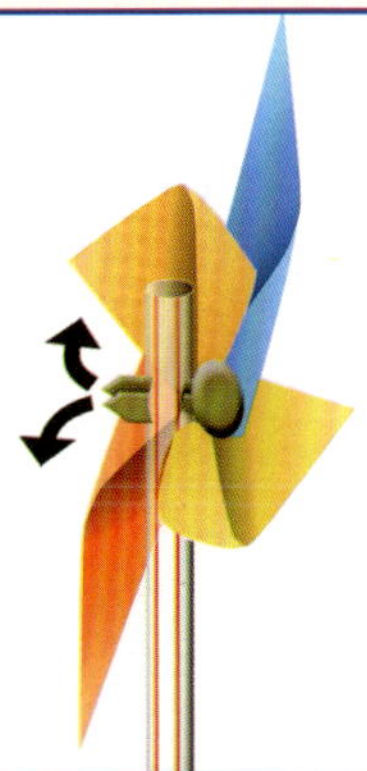

9

# Glossary

**atoms**—basic building blocks of all matter

**electrons**—basic particles, each carrying one unit of negative charge

**engineers**—people who plan, build, or manage a project

**force**—a push or pull that makes things move

**inclined plane**—a simple machine for elevating or lowering objects

**lever**—a simple machine that makes work easier by multiplying the force put into it

**magnetism**—an invisible force that pushes or pulls

**motion**—a change in position

**pole**—the end of a magnet

**prototype**—a model of a new object

**pulley**—a simple machine with a wheel over which a rope, belt, chain, or cable runs to make it easier to lift heavy objects

**repel**—to push away

**screw**—a threaded spiral pin or rod used as a simple machine to attach or build objects

**simple machine**—a machine that uses one movement to make work easier

**wedge**—the pointed edge of an inclined plane that can be used to push things apart

**wheel and axle**—a round ring with spokes that turns a post attached to it, causing movement

**work**—force moving an object

# Index

# Scientists Then and Now

**Augusta Ada King,**
**Countess of Lovelace**
**(1815–1852)**

Countess Lovelace is best known for thinking up the "analytical engine." It was an early model computer. She wrote a complete set of instructions for the engine. Her instructions are considered to be the world's first computer program!

**Chavon Grande**
**(1978– )**

Chavon Grande is an engineer. Engineers design and build things. Amusement park rides are just one type of thing that Grande has made! Today, she designs many kinds of structures. One of her main jobs is to be sure that the structures protect and respect the environment.

## Image Credits

Cover charles taylor/Shutterstock; p.1 charles taylor/Shutterstock; p.4 Gusto/Photo Researchers, Inc.; p.4-5 Gusto/Photo Researchers, Inc.; p.5 KRT/Newscom; p.6-7 Roger L./UPI Photo/Newscom; p.7 PRISMA/Newscom; p.8-9(top) NASA; p.8-9 Cordelia Molloy/Photo Researchers, Inc.; p.8 Morgan Lane Photography/Shutterstock; p.10-11 Charles D. Winters/Photo Researchers, Inc.; p.10 Franck Boston/Shutterstock; p.11(top) Tim Bradley; p.11(bottom) Mauro Fermariello/Photo Researchers, Inc.; p.12 David R. Frazier Photolibrary, Inc./Alamy; p.13 empipe/Shutterstock; p.14-15 Tim Bradley; p.14-15(bottom) TongRo Image Stock/Alamy; p.15 iStockphoto; p.16 Katrina Brown/Shutterstock; p.17(left) Fanfo/Shutterstock; p.17 Don Tran/Shutterstock; p.18 (bottom) Lara Barrett/Shutterstock; p.17-18 Ed Bock/CORBIS; p.19 STILLFX/Shutterstock; p.20(top) Tom O'Connell/Alamy; p.20 Adrov Andriy/Shutterstock; p.20-21 as-foto/Shutterstock; p.22-23(bottom) charles taylor/Shutterstock; p.23 Leonard Lessin/Photo Researchers, Inc.; p.22-23 Sheila Terry/Photo Researchers, Inc.; p.24-25(top) Andraž Cerar/Shutterstock; p.24-25(bottom) Tim Bradley; p.25 David Young-Wolff/Alamy; p.26-27 Philippe Psaila/Photo Researchers, Inc.; p.26-27(bottom) The Granger Collection, New York; p.29 kazberry/Shutterstock; p.32(left) National Physical Gallery, Teddington; p.32(right) Rick Reason